<u>Advance Praise for Nuggets</u>

'Nuggets' well exceeded my expectations! Not that I anticipated something less, but this book's simplistic, yet profound presentation brought many parcels of wisdom and axioms to light for me, that I'm sure you will experience too. If you love dogs, you will love this book. If you are fascinated with leadership, you will love this book. If you happen be so fortunate to treasure both, well, you are in for a real treat (pun intended) and indulgence. Caz has a God-given talent that has allowed him to merge dog training and discipline with tested and true leadership principles, that will be easily remembered by the reader, forever.'
Doug Savidge, Owner / CEO
Action Coach - Lewisburg

"Caz Russell has done an outstanding job sharing his insights in leadership that he learned from training his dogs. Anyone reading this book will learn insights and grow in the personal life."
Robert A. Rohm, Ph.D.
President, Personality Insights, Inc.

"Leadership lessons exist everywhere in the world around us. Caz (Nuggets) provides a unique and entertaining way to look at leadership – through the eyes of a trainer and his dog. Many times, throughout this book I found myself fondly remembering the dogs who have been a part of my life and the lessons they humbly taught me."
Bruce Mellott
Vice President Safety
Asplundh Tree Expert, LLC

NUGGETS

WHAT TRAINING MY DOGS HAS TAUGHT ME ABOUT LIFE & LEADERSHIP!

CAZ RUSSELL

DEDICATION

This book is dedicated to the dog trainer who has left an unforgettable impact on my life. Without him, I would not be the person I am today and would not be able to affect so many others by using my dog stories to help others learn how to grow their leadership skills. Thank you, Jim Seibel.

ACKNOWLEDGMENTS

I've learned many skills throughout my lifetime. How to run a newspaper route, clean office buildings, morning milk deliveries, maintaining a mail route at the local factory to coaching high school students, stocking grocery shelves, generate electricity, and my favorite skill - dog training.

Through all the years I've had many coaches, mentors and trainers teach me what, how and why to perform my duties at a high standard.

No one has encouraged me more than my wife, Diane Savidge Russell. We are about as opposite as one can imagine. Which is just what I needed to learn to become the husband, father, speaker and writer that I am becoming.

I would also like to thank Tim Schulte and *Variance Author Services* for taking such great care of me, as a first-time author. Tim's help has made this a better book. Special thanks as well to the talented Mirjana Krasojevic for the amazing cover art and Sharon K Merkel LLC for the beautiful drawing of Caz's dogs.

NUGGETS

PREFACE

I'm not sure what first attracted me to dogs. Their usefulness on this planet is immeasurable. No other animal has taught me how to become a leader more than my six dogs. Dogs bring to every relationship love, comfort, adoration, healing and so much more.

Although I have yet to find any breed of dog which does not appeal to me, the foundation of this book is built on a dog named Oats, a Labrador retriever, which had no equal in her desire, drive and love for retrieving. Unfortunately, this very large, yellow Labrador retriever, had the misfortune to have me as her master and leader.

I had no experience in general dog obedience training let alone understanding the fundamentals of teaching a dog how to retrieve. Yet, I did learn, mainly because of my good fortune to have a dog like her. She taught me more about leadership than I ever could have learned from a book.

This journey has been enlightening; from our very first Labrador retriever, Cooper, then Levi, then Oats to our current dogs, Chilli, Huckleberry and Sanford (a Havanese). These six faithful companions and I have spent countless hours over a thirty-year span, walking, running, swimming and most importantly, learning together.

Through the help and training of my dogs, I have compiled nineteen Nuggets of Leadership to help each of us learn and apply principles that will help us be more successful and better leaders to those we associate with. As you read it, highlight what works for you and ignore what doesn't. It's my sincere prayer and hope that all who utilize the Nuggets from this book in their everyday lives as I did might become the leaders they are meant to be.

"Inch by inch, it's a cinch, yard by yard it's very hard!" I encourage you to learn with me on this leadership journey. A journey of ups and downs, failure and achievements, happiness and sadness, but always learning forward to reach our full potential.

NUGGET # 1

WHAT WE ALLOW, WE TEACH!

I didn't know where my wife and I were headed in the early days of raising a puppy. In order to get a head start on what I was soon to learn, I purchased books on dog obedience training.

My first introduction to our new houseguest was a rude awakening that the pup would claim every room for his personal bathroom. We soon learned to close off all rooms we didn't want Oats, our third

1

Labrador retriever, to visit. Our next mission was to remove all items which normally were left on the floor. Shoes and clothes were somehow disappearing from their normal resting place. Often, we found them hours later in a completely different condition. At times it seemed easier to let the puppy have her way.

Through our dog's behavior and my response to it, I learned Nugget # 1:

"WHAT WE ALLOW, WE TEACH!"

2

If I allow my dog to do an unwanted behavior, I have taught her that behavior. Without addressing an undesirable behavior like jumping up on us or bolting out the door without permission, these habits become the norm.

Dr. Phil tells us, "We teach people how to treat us!" By allowing our children to beg, cry and whine for ice cream actually teaches them this unfavorable act. Once you apply this nugget to all areas of your life, you will see just how easy it is to shape the behavior of not only your dog, but that of people with whom you live, work and play. I have found this nugget to be helpful in almost every area of my life.

After spending 5 years in an office administrative position just out of high school, I was blessed to be hired by the electric power company. I will never forget that first day, showing up at the coal fired power plant in docker dress pants, double knit shirt and Acme dingo boots. I must have looked like someone who belonged in an office and not in a power plant. A coal fired power plant is truly an amazing creature. This power plant was 150 feet high and its footprint on the ground equaled 4 football fields. The main building held nine floors above the ground and two floors below ground level. It took approximately 5 minutes to walk from the parking lot to the main administrative building. I clearly remember walking into my supervisor's office at 7:00am reporting for duty, and he firmly and gruffly told me to report to the Lead Handyman for job instructions.

It must have been customary for those that had worked at the plant for some time, to initiate the new hires. With me being clean shaven and dressed like an office worker, their eyes told me, this was going to be brutal, and it was. One could only sit in the break room at an unassigned seat. Assigned seats were only assigned to a worker because of their seniority, or as they told me *"I have always sat here and I will always sit here during every break, lunch and rest period!"* I did as they told me to, as I found a very old metal seat that looked like it did not belong to anyone and claimed it for mine. Some gents put their names or their nicknames on their seats with magic marker and some kept their lunch pails on the table in front of their seats clearly defining ownership. These aluminum pails were most likely used for the many years one would be working. They just didn't wear out and often looked like New York City taxis with all the dings, dents and scrapes.

It took several days until I realized that if I didn't stand up to the old guard, they would rule over me forever, with good or bad intentions. I decided I would listen to the old guard which is my natural way. In my heart, I knew that sooner or later, I would need to stand up for myself and not allow others to treat me in a way that was arrogant but respectful. Growing up in central Pennsylvania, which is a very rural area, most people worked at factories, farms or in the coal mines, which of course, supplied the fuel to the fossil fuel plants. These power plant workers were dedicated, hard workers willing to work in very unhealthy environments. As each new day brought new challenges and situations, I kept falling back on "what we allow, we teach!" If I allow a co-worker to treat me with disrespect, I am teaching that co-worker that disrespectful behavior is acceptable. I immediately need to address the situation by confronting the behavior, face to face, rather than letting the conflict grow out of hand and become the norm.

Probably the hardest part of dog training for me, was being consistent. Every time my dog began an unwanted behavior, I needed to address it, immediately. Being consistent in my dog training meant that every time I give my dog the "Here" command, the dog needs to obey 100% of the time. Not sometimes, not most times, not once in a while, but every time. This consistency builds the format for working together. If I give my dog the "Here" command and he doesn't obey, then I am the one who is at fault. When in doubt whether your dog will listen or not, put a check cord on them, then you will be able to control their actions This check cord is a rope usually ten to 50 feet in length and has a brass clip on one end which attaches to your dog while the other end is maintained by the dog handler.

I understand we can't put a check cord on co-workers or family, although, some try, we need to be consistent with our intentions, our words and our actions. This is really the backbone of "What we allow, we teach!" Addressing an unwanted behavior every time and in real time.

8

NUGGET # 2

WHEN TO APPLY CORRECTION

My desire to train Labrador retrievers did not begin until we purchased Oats, our third yellow Labrador retriever, as a family and hunting dog. Over the next few months, Oats, grew and learned very fast. Nothing stays in proportion as a Lab puppy grows. That breed's feet are much larger than all other body parts, evidenced by their unusual and clumsy maneuvers by walking into doors before they are

9

opened. Without the dog's very large landing pads, she wouldn't have been able to handle her crazy attempts to reach the sofa.

Whether it's a dog's enthusiasm, their desire to be the highest object in the room, or a temporary loss of thought process, I will never understand why they attempt to do the impossible.

My response is Nugget # 2:

"WHEN TO APPLY CORRECTION"

Have you ever pleaded and begged your dog to come to you, but twenty minutes passes by before he decides to obey? When coming to your side, the dog looks at you with eyes that say, "I am sorry. Were you talking to me?"

Unfortunately, the time for correction is long overdue. Correction should have been applied as soon as there was a refusal to obey. Walking to the dog and making him obey instantly will gain the desired result.

If you wait to apply the correction once the pup has finally decided to obey, he often becomes confused and misinterprets the correction as discipline. Both you and your dog will be frustrated and he might never learn the command. Correction is neither punishment nor discipline for a dog or a human. My goal of correction is helping someone to improve. Much like dog training, without addressing

11

the need to change when the act is performed, continued disappointment is often the result.

This principle really popped out at me when I applied it to the rating reports, I used to evaluate employee performance. The time to address an incorrect behavior or action is at the time of the event, not days, weeks, months or even years later. You might be surprised how often this happens in our relationships at work now that I have brought it to your attention.

I can remember very clearly while sitting in tailboard before the beginning of our work shift, co-workers venting their frustrations with personal attacks on others, especially if said person was not in the room. Unacceptable behavior? You bet! Do I let these negative comments drive the day's events, or do I address them either in the room in front of everyone or outside the meeting, as a one-on-one conversation? This timing factor builds trust between yourself as a leader and others around us. In "The 21 Irrefutable Laws of Leadership" by John C. Maxwell, John states when we give correction or feedback is just as important as "how and where we give feedback or correction."

Giving constructive feedback is crucial and even more helpful when it comes soon after the event. Co-workers often hold ill will against others, with no intention of forgiving or forgetting the situation or behavior. Carrying around this burden without addressing it face to face, we find ourselves never letting go and moving past the event. Who suffers the most when wrongs are not forgiven or negative feelings exist? We do, not the other person, just us. I find it amazing how one can remember every last detail of the wrongdoing, but when we truly forgive others, it becomes another circumstance or experience in our life that we choose to grow from. One that doesn't hold a high priority or top of mind place in our emotions.

This same principle is so vitally important outside of work, with our families and friends. We as grandparents might be more willing to live with the unacceptable behavior in our grandchildren as we often put off when to correct, for many different reasons period. Whether addressing a selfish behavior,

14

an unexpected tantrum or teaching the importance of telling the truth, I need to ask myself this question. "Do I give correction immediately or is it better to let both parties think about the consequences of their actions, before a discussion is held."

I think it's important here to add that there is a substantial difference between criticism and feedback. Criticism carries with it a theory of negativity and disapproval, while feedback should be given and received with an atmosphere for improvement and growth. I often find people perceive that these two words have the same meaning, which they really do not. Unsolicited criticism is like a drive by shooting. Without asking permission to share your criticism, do we really know if the other person wants or is willing to listen to it? Whereas when a relationship is built, and feedback is an agreed upon item by both sides, each of us learns and grows. The person receiving feedback needs to listen, apply and change. The person giving feedback needs to be intentional about what they are trying to achieve with others and they need to share in a way that connects with the receiver.

NUGGET # 3

ENFORCING A

COMMAND

After a few months of general obedience training, I began to think this dog training stuff wasn't very difficult. I decided to make a visit to my dog mentor's training facility and show him how well Oats and I were progressing in her retriever skills. At that time, I felt proud of what the two of us had accomplished. However, I soon learned the most

17

influential and valuable nugget for dog training and for life.

After teaching a dog the basic obedience commands such as sit, off, no/no and stay, the command "Here!" is the most important and hardest to install in a dog's understanding.

Thus, Nugget # 3:

"ENFORCING A COMMAND"

In the beginning stages of the pup's training, the commands have required your dog to obey most of the time. As your new best friend is now learning

18

more and more lessons, the command "Here!" must not be the one the dog will obey when she feels like it.

If I call my dog twenty times to come, then my dog has "taught me" that I must say the command twenty times until she decides to obey. I came to realize that part of the training must be in my court. I need to control my verbal commands to not only stop repeating the command over and over but also to just not give the command "sometimes" because I knew the dog would not respond correctly at that time.

I started to use this same principle when it came to having my grandchildren pick up their toys at the end of their visit. I needed to learn to only tell them "twice" to pick up their toys. Maybe they didn't hear me on the first time, so I am willing to repeat the

19

direction due to them possibly not hearing me well. But that's it, only twice. Upon finding that they possibly are going to not follow my directions, I immediately went to them and we picked up the toys together. I am willing to pitch in and help if it helps them understand what "pap" is expecting of them, but I do not do all of the work.

When we enforce our commands, we set the stage for expectations. A lack of communication should never be the reason for the job at hand not being accomplished. When a command isn't followed, I must first ask myself "What did I do wrong?" and not "What are they doing wrong?" This consistency is amazingly hard, but so very important in growing as a leader. Remember how I told you how proud I was after several weeks of intensive training and then having the opportunity to show my mentor how good we were doing. Well, that balloon burst very fast on that day. Upon taking Oats from the training kennel into the field, I gave her the command to fetch an object that my partner had thrown. I will never forget her racing at full breakneck speed after the thrown object. This was a simple 100-yard retrieve, over some dirt mounds and thru some weeds. Not much of a challenge for a well-trained retriever.

Oats was about to hit the 50-yard mark on her 100-yard retrieve, when something clicked in her brain. Actually, it was in her nose. Ahh, the scent of a fresh partridge in the brush. She never broke stride, never looked back and never did find that bumper.

She only wanted the most tantalizing smell she had ever discovered and this partridge was not in a pear tree. It was on the ground and making tracks for the nearest burrow it could find. Oats never did find the bird and the lesson here to be learned was really about my consistency of enforcing a command. I kept yelling, yep, you guessed it "here, here, here, here, here" at least 20 times until I got tired of yelling the command. She was so far out into the field, I don't think she even heard me, and if she did, she was ignoring me. I looked over at Jim, he didn't smile, he didn't get emotional and with the most appropriate words to me he said, "If your dog doesn't come to you on the 20th time you give the command, she is not coming period, go get your dog, now!" It is a moment that will stick with me forever. I couldn't enforce my command for Oats to come here. I had no way of catching, stopping or having her come back to me. We had trained for many, hard, long hours on the "here command", but here she was doing exactly what she wanted to do. What a lesson!

We must set the standard from the very start, the very first event and every time after that when training our pup or our people until they are "rock" steady with commands or instructions. Timing is everything in dog training and life. Knowing when to give the command and knowing that you can enforce it, creates relationships that are built on trust.

23

NUGGET # 4

WHAT GETS PRAISED, GETS

REPEATED!

I never realized the importance of praising my dog upon completion of a trained behavior until she started lying beside me and looking at me with those sad and adoring eyes that said, *"Are you happy with me?"*

I'm not suggesting you always praise your pup when she finally decides to obey. It's just as important to withhold praise at the appropriate time as it is to praise them when they have done the exercise well. Timing is everything.

As I trained Chilli to retrieve the training bumper, it became apparent that my pockets were not big enough to hold the number of treats to match the number of times I wanted her to retrieve the object.

Enter Nugget # 4:

"WHAT GETS PRAISED, GETS REPEATED!"

After several weeks, then months of both of us connecting on a new level, I noticed she wanted to be near me all the time. We had built a relationship which

26

was more important than the task or goals I had set for us. As she learned that her repeat obedience brought praise, our relationship grew stronger, even to the point of becoming a deep, loyal friendship. Each of us couldn't have been happier.

In your relationships with families, friends, neighbors, and others you meet, applying the principles of this lesson will develop not only correct responses but also a loyalty that all those involved will treasure.

Have you ever noticed how much your loved one's love to receive a compliment from you? Whether it is their new hairstyle, new clothing outfit or maybe even that special meal they prepared just the way you like it. A few simple compliments really mean a lot to the person on the receiving end. They realize that the person giving the praise is actually paying attention to the details. It also shows that the person giving the praise has taken time out of their schedule to invest in someone else. After 46 years of marriage, I finally learned what really means the most to my wife. It's not fancy clothes, jewelry or even a date night. What matters most to her is that I have taken the time to focus solely on her. No interruptions, no being too busy to give her my full attention and notice what is really important to her. This is where "what gets praised, gets repeated" really comes into play. I need to know what she likes and doesn't like. She likes a complete timeout on my part and totally being in the moment with her, whether at the dinner table or on the sofa or just sitting on the front porch.

When it comes to praise, I have found none who do not like it. Oh, some may say they don't need it, but deep inside their soul, their very core, we all love praise. We want to know that we are liked, needed and appreciated. Yes, the same goes for our family canine companion. Treats are a very useful tool in getting your dog to learn tricks, games and behaviors. But praise, really brings it to their inner being. A treat lasts but a few seconds in the mouth, but when they receive your praise and you are letting them know they are the best dog in the world, you are establishing a lifelong relationship of trust and love.

So, how do I praise my dog upon completion of a desired behavior? For my labs, they love a good, hearty thump on their chest along with a big smile and attaboy, even if it's a girl dog. I was amazed when I began to understand how much they associate to their human with the use of their eyes and ears. Add to praise a good healthy rub on the head, and their world has now become even better due to someone taking the time to praise them.

Learning what to say and when to say it, is our responsibility. We need to be intentional about the praise we give by making it specific, not just a generic "well-done or good job!" Learn to identify what it is that you are going to praise and set time aside to do it in the proper atmosphere. Be in the moment. Praising someone a week later could mean one is just trying to play catch up. Or, praising too soon, could project to them that its automatic and very insincere.

30

The bottom line is when we praise others for what they are doing or have done; we will actually encourage them to be successful again. The person receiving praise will feel empowered, appreciated, important and valued. Each of us have an innate desire to be needed.

NUGGET # 5

"TRAIN A FAST DOG SLOW AND A SLOW DOG FAST!"

It's amazing how much energy puppies have. Like our children, they play hard and fast, and all of a sudden you find them sleeping in the most unusual places and positions. As they grow, their behavior changes as fast as their physical growth.

It's very difficult to determine at which point a puppy changes to the adult stage. Some Labs seem to be puppy's even at the age of eight.

As we train our companions, there is a visible turnover from immaturity and enthusiasm to knowledge and a work-like-a-dog attitude.

Every dog, no matter what the breed, have their own unique personalities, behaviors and genetic makeup. Some may like to bark, some like to run, some like to lie on your lap, while others simply are content to lie at your feet. The key to helping each one become the best dog he can be is for us to know how to connect with him.

Let's look at Nugget # 5:

"TRAIN A FAST DOG SLOW AND A SLOW DOG FAST!"

If my dog is a strong-willed "I'd rather do it my way" laid back kind of dog, I'll bring more enthusiasm to his training than normal. Vice versa, if the pup wants to go, go and go some more, always ready to run, I'd slow down his training. I'll teach the pup in a very methodical step by step process while trying to bring the excitement level down. If my training buddy is sluggish and lazy, I pick up the pace and build some excitement and enthusiasm. I want to be in control of the training not just because I am the teacher, trainer or master. I also want the pup to learn what is and what is not acceptable behavior.

Let's apply this leadership principle to the workforce we live in daily. Upon training a new employee for their job position, it's important that we

35

train in a way that connects with the person's personality. When a new employee comes on board, it's important not to speed ahead too fast with instructions that may hinder their learning process. However, if proceeding too slowly, the trainee could get bored and begin to disconnect.

Great leaders connect with others at the speed of their learning, at their speed of absorption of practices and procedures. What we are trying to achieve here is providing an environment for them to feel safe and that is conducive to their learning the tasks at hand. Not everyone learns at the same speed and rhythm. Our goal as a leader is to give the employee the best opportunity at succeeding in their new position. In today's world, we need to not only find and train employees but also to retrain them. If by chance, they decide to leave and pursue a new or different career, we have done the right thing for them and for our company.

Let's analyze this a bit further. Say I have a dog that continually jumps up when he sees me or others and often knocks their new acquaintance down or worse. Our dog is excited and so very happy, but he has let his emotions win over his controlled behaviors. See the parallel? This Nugget really comes down to emotional control, both ours and the new trainee, whether it be a dog or a person. First, I need to understand how my emotions affect the training situation. Then, I need to understand the emotions of the trainee. This takes time and effort. This takes a relationship. I need to know what their needs are and what drives them or makes them tick. What gets their learning stimulus working on all four cylinders, as my father would say.

Next, I need to prepare myself on which techniques I need to apply which will help each of us be successful in their training. Each of us needs to prepare ourselves before the training begins. A power plant is a very noisy place, extremely noisy, ok, it's not a good environment for training on the job. If I expect someone to walk alongside huge motors, blowers and fans and expect them to learn, it's just not going to happen. Much will be lost in the transmission of information.

"*Leadership is always an inside job*" – *John C. Maxwell*

The connection between me and the one learning is my responsibility. If I choose not to connect, then the problem is on me, but if the other one chooses not to connect, then the problem is on them.

As Zig Ziglar would say "I need to plan, prepare and expect to win!" And by win, I mean that both the dog handler and the dog learn to work as one. The same nugget applies in leadership with the mentor/mentee relationship, for those who I intentionally want to help train, educate and inspire to be their best.

39

NUGGET # 6

NO, NO DRILL!

Our neighbor once told me that he thought my new puppy's name was "No" because I was constantly yelling the word at a very high pitch. I am guessing my voice probably travelled for many blocks in our small community. I soon learned that yelling and screaming only made my throat sore and annoyed the neighbors. I came to realize I was actually teaching my dog to ignore me. Yelling creates disobedience and like people, a dog learns to ignore the given directions. My mentor taught me that intimidation, manipulation and

41

force does not build trust between a dog and their owner.

Then, Nugget # 6 came to mind.

"NO, NO DRILL!"

A dog can learn over fifty words. Why not use that to both his advantage and mine.

Teaching mans' best friend as many words as you can, creates an atmosphere of trust, obedience and repetition. Without yelling at the pup to stop an unwanted behavior, I simply taught him the words "no, no!" These were a powerful set of words that accomplished correction without fear. I wanted my pup to be obedient not because of fear but because he trusted me.

Coming home from a long, hard day at work, I found myself raising my voice to match my emotions. Rather than raising my voice to an extremely high pitch, I needed to be calm, cool and even tempered when telling my sons, "No, you can't do that!" when they were in a heated argument which led to angry tempers and more. I became much more effective as a leader when my emotions and the tone of my voice were under my control. The result being that both the children and the dogs responded in a more positive "happy" way.

I will never forget our first yellow male Labrador retriever, Cooper. One weekend afternoon, the family found him emptying his stomach onto the linoleum floor in the kitchen. One's first reaction was to think that we now have a sick dog. But upon inspecting the kitchen table, I found the butter dish completely empty. Yep, one half pound of butter gone in an instant. Evidently the butter didn't sit well with him and up it came. He did recover nicely that evening, but we did constantly have to keep the butter dish concealed from a very ingenious and hungry lab.

In the days that followed, the whole family found themselves yelling the word "No" every time Cooper got near the kitchen table. I soon realized it was time to change my language, communication and training. I worked very hard over the next several weeks to stop yelling the word "No" and began to utilize different words that would be effective.

As the years progressed and with more dogs that we added to our family history, I found it took a dedicated effort on my part to be clear, concise, effective, efficient, and courteous. I needed to learn to not use my old standby words of communication and use verbal language in a way that helped me connect with my dogs. To help each of our dogs to become the best they could be, I needed to change the way I communicated. We will talk more about body language ahead, but for now, like a dog bone hidden in the ground, let's uncover some words which may help each of us to not be "Lazy in Communication!"

It's amazing how each of us learn our behaviors due to our environment. I often find myself saying the same thing my father or grandfather would say. These phrases or quips really stick many years later, and somehow seemed appropriate to say, at least at the moment and in my mind. Phrases like *"the faster I go, the more behinder I get"*, *"if you don't listen, I will put a tin ear on you"* and *"would you like a swift kick in the butt, son?"* Jim Rohn tells us "Don't be lazy with language!" The more words each of us learn, the better communicators we become. I can remember years ago being encouraged to read the Readers' Digest and in it was a section entitled "Word Power Quiz." In my teenage years, I would think who really cares about these words that most people have never seen, read or spoken. But now, I find myself trying to not be lazy in communication. Learning and adding new words to our vocabulary enables each of us to broaden our horizons, exist during unusual situations and even help each of us improve our people skills.

When we learn and apply more to our vocabulary, we are enabling ourselves to be more effective communicators which improves our leadership skills. This doesn't mean we need to learn very complicated words and phrases. I am suggesting we build our word vocabulary each day by adding to the already existing data base.

To this day, I am amazed at how my children have learned their leadership skills by watching me. Intentionally, I need to take ownership of my life, my actions and my words. "When I grow, everything around me grows!"

NUGGET # 7

ALWAYS END WITH A SUCCESS

There doesn't seem to be any age of a dog when they do not like to succeed. Maybe it's because they know we are happy with them or perhaps, they know their actions are very pleasing to us.

Every training exercise should have a beginning, some sort of performance, and an ending. With the beginning, I want to make sure what I want the dog to learn. The second part is to actually have my dog experience the training exercise. Upon completion of the exercise, whether it went well or not so well, I always want to end the dog training

49

exercise with a success, a win. It's been my goal to never end a training regimen without the dog knowing he did well.

Nugget # 7:

"ALWAYS END WITH A SUCCESS!"

Whether we're teaching word or whistle commands, hand signals or fun tricks around the house, I have found it very important to end with a win. At the end of every training event, we want our pup to walk away knowing his master is very happy with him and that he accomplished something great. This keeps him coming back for more. More training, more learning, more fun and more love. When the next training session arrives, he will be ready and willing to experience success again.

As an amateur dog trainer, I found myself wanting to train more and more, and as I watched my Labs begin to really catch on to this training regiment, I discovered the more I helped them learn, the more they wanted to learn and the more I learned. A dog sleeps much better when he knows he is loved, appreciated, trusted and has succeeded in his mentor's eyes.

Each of us is created with an innate desire to be appreciated and respected. With co-workers, friends and family, an encouraging word and a simple pat on the back or "Thank you!" may just be the words that a person needs to hear to make their day.

51

The secret to successful training and growth is to end on a successful note. We need to see each training session end with a win/win. Did you ever hear someone say, "this is my last ski run for the day?", only to break a leg on their final run. Brings a negative to the whole day of learning and fun, doesn't it? For whatever reason, we are tired, not paying attention or just letting loose, this last run more often ends in tragedy. Here in Pennsylvania, we seldom get a snowfall like the big ski states. Instead of skiing on several feet of powder, we most often are skiing on slopes that are packed harder than a major interstate highway. We often find ourselves snow skating rather than snow skiing. If only the skier stopped when he chose to, rather than when they had to.

I found this principle very applicable not only in skiing and dog training but also in developing our leadership skills. As we grow and as we help others grow their leadership skills, we want to realize that each person learns at the rate of how they succeed. When success is achieved, we need to realize and celebrate those successes.

Take for instance, teaching my grandson to mow the grass. He comes to me and asks, "how can I make some money?" Well now, I believe I like that attitude. Now it's time to get the old thinkin noggin workin. Let's apply his desire to make money to learn a new skill. This skill might be physical but it also has leadership principles that one can apply.

I went about showing him how to check the lawnmowers oil and gas. Taught him how the blade works and how dangerous it is and gave him the proper protective goggles and hearing protection and then instructed him how this mower works. How to start it, how to stop it and which flowers are allowed to be mowed over and which ones aren't. He was definitely more excited than I was at this point of his learning. He saw clouds of money while I saw a possible monetary loss in the mower being damaged as well as Mimi's flowers.

After the instructions were given, off he went mowing the grass of our one-third acre of mostly flat lawn, which really is a benefit for a first-time lawnmower. I proceeded to my Lazy Boy for an afternoon nap while he took on the task at hand like a sixteen-year-old with a driver's license permit. He was excited. Now I must say that he was way more mature than I was at the age of 14. If I had applied my apprehensions to him that my father had of me, well, I believe I would have been standing guard from the patio. Nope, off to my favorite chair, which every grandfather has. The one nobody sits in except Pap.

I would occasionally hear the mower blade hitting hard objects like rocks, but all in all, he did great. Coming back in after about 60 minutes, he proudly says "Pap, I am done!" His smile was just a tad bit bigger than mine, but believe me, inside I was beaming. This young man performed his assignment just as I had hoped. No damage and no flowers were destroyed. He went home that day with a great sense of satisfaction and confidence. He was ready for his next challenge.

As we are helping others to grow their leadership skills, we need to realize that each person learns at a rate of how they fail and succeed. When they do succeed, realize and celebrate that success. Such was the case with my grandson. By empowering him, his ownership and responsibility grew larger and I learned how to better influence others by having faith in them.

NUGGET # 8

TUG OF WAR

Seems like a simple game, doesn't it? Take one of Pap's old holey socks, tie a knot on each end. One for you to hold and one for your new best friend to grab, and let the games begin.

If you've ever done this with your beloved dog, did you notice the man rugs turned upside down in your living room? It's amazing to watch how a dog figures out if she puts her feet on the rug, she gets much more "gription." (This word used often by a friend, says its half grip and half traction – gription).

57

As much as my dog and I loved playing this game, it was important for the dog to learn not to play this game. Why? Tug of War immediately instills in a dog a "them versus us" mentality, a mine and I want you to try and get it from me mindset.

I was amazed when I realized the importance of Nugget # 8:

"TUG OF WAR!"

Learning this principle very quickly, without the pup even thinking about it, she immediately applied it to many other areas of her world.

This behavior also instills a hierarchy between you and your four-legged friend. Defeating you in Tug of War creates in the dog's mind that she is superior, she has won and will always win. This behavior is not what we are attempting to achieve.

When training your retriever to bring you the object of desire on command, there is often an adversarial relationship. Occasionally, the pup will go for the object you have thrown and then stand there and look at you as if to say "It's mine, come and get it if you think you are fast enough!"

From the start of the relationship, I want the pup to know we are a team. Once the pup understands this principle, our teamwork grows and so does our relationship.

It is the same with us.

59

Watching on TV the Tug of War rope battles at the beach, one can easily see the natural desire to win in people. Unfortunately, with this battle being waged, one side wins and one side loses. However, when each side sees the other as supportive, encouraging and helpful, both sides achieve success.

Several years ago, some members of the church, where my wife and I attend came to me with an idea of starting a men's small group. As many of you might realize, men not just women, have a need to have someone listen to their thoughts, worries, concerns and more. This became a very exciting experience for me as I was asked to be the leader of the group. I quickly accepted the invitation, due to understanding that there is a huge need for us gentleman to open up our hearts to others.

This adventure began with lots of prayer and advice from my wife and the pastor. I needed to figure out a way to build trust with these gentlemen and also to create an environment of cooperation. Not easy when you have men from all walks of life, different backgrounds and different cultures. If you have ever noticed, when two dogs meet, there is a natural pecking order going on. Each dog is checking the other dog out with the use of eye contact, their proud stance and some internal growling. As I introduced myself to many men in the church and invited them to this newly formed team, it was apparent that meeting complete strangers I was having much the same experience. Each of us wanted to know who was alpha and who was the beta "dog."

Falling back on what I learned from my mentor, was that teams are built on trust. As this team's newly appointed leader, working very hard on this principle became my # 1 priority. Teams do not perform and accomplish great things without trust and I was the one who needed to lead by example and that isn't always easy. For this team of men to function and grow, each person needed to value each other for who they are, period. We didn't need any "Tug of War" between each other. To accomplish this my goal was to provide an environment of honesty and integrity. As my father would say "easier said than done!"

Now trust is not built overnight. "Trust comes from consistency and competency, "said the US commander of the Gulf War, General H. Arnold Schwarzkopf. From the beginning, my main focus for these gentlemen was not to give or tell the answers to life, but to have them open up and share with each other. The entire group of men together contained more knowledge, experience and wisdom than I could even imagine. My role was to facilitate weekly discussion on our faith, family and the challenges each of us have at their current stages of our lives. Boy, did I get what I asked for! I must say this experience was much needed for all of us and over time, acquaintances became allies, allies became friends and several small inner circles were developed which created even more growth for everyone.

NUGGET # 9

MAKE IT STICK

The word "stick" might bring to mind a branch from a tree or even a tree limb, the perfect one, which pup always seems to find to play with. A dog can search through thousands of branches in the woods and always seems to find, at least in his mind, the stick that has just the right odor, shape and texture to retrieve.

Whether the dog is small or large, thick or thin, the retriever will either bring the stick to its human or just run with it in his mouth, not caring if it's eight inches or eight feet in length. With the stick in his

65

mouth sideways, he could possibly hit every obstacle in his path, which jars his teeth, mouth and entire body while he runs impervious to his surroundings. At that moment, the stick means everything to that dog.

Very often, I will find pup running as fast as he can in an effort to get to the other end of the field, only to see them make a huge looping circle and return just as fast as when they took off. Why? No one knows. They just love to run and there is something about retrievers in the recesses of their brain, that more than anything, they want an object in their mouth. How do they run this way? Why do they run this way? What are they trying to achieve? When will they tire of running and carrying this object? My guess is they will run as long as they can.

I learned in a most unfortunate way, Nugget # 9:

"MAKE IT STICK!"

As Huckleberry, our fifth Labrador retriever in the Russell family tree, ran in glee with what was nothing but a small log, he came racing up behind me as the branch hit me behind the knees, knocking me down so quickly that I couldn't protect myself. Looking up from my fallen position, my legs hurting, my emotions boiling and thoughts running through my mind. My first thought was "What hit me?" which led to my second thought "When I catch you!" Will I remember one of the most physically painful days of my life? You bet? Will he? Probably not. At this point in time, he came to me and sat there dropping the

67

stick in front of me as if to say "What is wrong, are you okay, did you fall, what happened to you?"

In making memories with Huck, the term "Make it Stick!" often comes to my mind in a most unpleasant way. From that time on, every learning session with any pup, every training event or memorable adventure, I needed to figure out a way to "Make it Stick!" in Huck's memory bank.

Relating this training principle to my own life, when events and experiences happen, the ones that stick are the ones that have had the most impact on my life. A lesson learned the hard way or a great memorable experience helps me recall and apply leadership principles.

As a youngster growing up in the 60's, 1960 that is, life was a lot different than in the 1990's, but then again, some things never change. Mom and Dad insisted that I went to the dentist for a checkup once a year. Somewhere in my very early teens, I will never forget one dentist visit, where I found out that I had seven cavities. You might be able to imagine the look on my face, as the report was given to myself and my parents. The dentist required I visit him every Thursday after school for seven weeks, and he would repair one filling at a time. Can you imagine a 13-year-old walking home from school and heading to downtown Milton, PA, so my dentist could practice his dentistry on me? I literally cried for the entire length of the walk.

I will never forget looking up into the glasses that the dentist wore and seeing the reflection of my teeth, tongue and mouth. Why do I remember this? Hey, I was 13 years old. Who knows? After the visit, I possibly had the emotion of someone winning the lottery. I was pain free for another 6 days. Who cares about tomorrow, right now, I feel good.

Fast forward to 2018, I am sitting in the dental chair and I ask the dental assistant, "When do you think people brush their teeth the most thorough?"

"Why the morning of their dental visit, of course!" she replied.

Thinking that this applies to most of us, my vision is of myself brushing away like crazy the morning before my checkup, now much older and with more gray hair.

Good dental care takes constant maintenance. Tartar and plaque are not removed in one brushing. Brushing needs to be a discipline that we turn into a behavior which we practice daily. Leadership is much the same way. We need to learn and apply leadership principles every day. To know what makes a great leader, we need to invest in ourselves every-day and keep a daily habit of reading information about what helps good leaders become great leaders. I need to refresh my thinking every day with thoughts and information that help build character, integrity, dependability and more.

Ever wonder how a joke starts in California and makes its way to Pennsylvania? Something "makes it stick." Someone who created the joke, shared it with others and they shared it with others. There is a connection, a trigger effect, an emotion that says, I will always remember this joke. Memorization is a great way to learn, but when we laugh, hurt, or help someone recover from a major mistake, it becomes a permanent tool to recall when necessary.

Like my earlier childhood dental story, which I believe will stick in your minds for quite some time, use stories like these to help others grow to their full potential. Leaders look for ways to "Make it Stick!" This means we must first be intentional about growing our own leadership skills in order to help others grow theirs. To make a point, tell a story. But… Make your story have a point.

NUGGET # 10

NEVER GIVE UP ON

YOUR DOG

Not every day that you train your pup is going to be the best day ever, neither for him nor for you. Some days, well, let's just say it's easier to sit on the couch than it is to put the effort forth with that hairy, jumping, running and gobbling everything in sight mischief maker.

In my case, it might be the weather, the location of training, or just my own state of mind. Some days I'm more interested in getting to the next project at home then teaching my loyal companion a new drill or behavior.

I came home one day from training Oats, our third Labrador retriever in the family tree and immediately told my wife that I had had enough. Oats was a very large, yellow female Labrador retriever, with the heart of a lion. On this day I believed the dog would not learn the behavior of staying in one spot for more than eight seconds.

While washing dishes, my dear wife looked me straight in the eyes, and said, "Everyone has a bad day once in a while!" Not every day does your dog give a hundred percent!

Her words struck a key thought with me and my dog training. Not every day, every moment, or event, do we have to complete the task immediately, almost supernaturally. Although I felt like quitting that day, my wife's simple reminder taught me an important lesson.

Nugget # 10 was born:

"NEVER GIVE UP ON YOUR DOG!"

Never give up on your dog should be the greatest truth in your arsenal. Returning the following day of a poor training episode, I found out that our pup was acting differently, she was acting like her "old self!" Even a dog has a bad day.

77

Likewise, whether working with dogs or with people, if you quit on them, they'll quit on you. How encouraging is it for those around us when we have an attitude that emits to them that no matter what the circumstances, you are not and will not give up on them.

In the late 1970's, my wife and I were Youth for Christ/Campus Life Directors for the local area high school in Milton, Pennsylvania. My wife and I began to meet with local senior high school students, in an effort to help guide them thru life with both a worldly vision and a faith based spiritual vision. This meant spending many hours with ninth thru twelfth grade students, boys and girls and finding new ways to build relationships in an effort to leave a lifetime impact on them, ones they would never forget.

One of our many adventures included yearly backpack trips to the mountains. Most years, all went fine and dandy, meaning, sunshine, warm weather and not too many dangers. On one such three-day weekend backpacking trip on the Black Forest trail in Pennsylvania, things did not quite go as planned. Now, as a so-called adult (22 to be exact) my wife and I put together a backpack trip for October, which normally in central Pennsylvania is a beautiful fall with leaves turning gold, chilly evenings and crispier mornings. As newbies to backpacking, we often went with meals that could be prepared in fifteen minutes or less, flannel shirts and jeans, and typical, everyday sneakers.

On this soon to be a horrendous, rainy, muddy and slippery backpacking trip of two adults and ten students, we were definitely not prepared for an eighteen-mile hike with two overnight stays in the pouring rain. Sleeping bags were completely soaked and heavy, all of our clothes were the same, there were not dry sets to change into. Worse yet, by Sunday morning, the small shallow creeks which one could step across on rocks, were now up to our waists when crossing. At the highest creek, we needed to make a human chain, like connecting monkeys in a barrel, just to get across.

What makes one person give up when the going gets tough and one person who will persevere? Attitude! Why does one person want to call it quits and go home? Attitude! What does a newbie and his wife do when ten students are wet, hungry, tired, in the mountains 10 miles from a vehicle or building and another sixty miles from home sweet home? Take ownership, own the circumstances and develop a plan to recover. The attitude of the followers always is an indication of the attitude of their leader/s.

Now, by no means am I a Bear Grylls type, or a survival instructor type. No physical or mental training, heck I don't know how to start a fire in a rainstorm or keep dry in the worst conditions. My only thought was my wife and these ten students were my responsibility and mine alone. There was no one else. Their parents were expecting me to bring them home safe like in a "Rambo" movie. What I did have to my advantage was an attitude as big as the challenge. I am not sure how I developed this attitude, maybe nature or nurture, but I have it. Always did, always will.

Zig Ziglar tells us *"A good attitude will not get you anything more than a bad attitude, but it will help you get everything more than a bad attitude!"* I could not make the rain stop, or ease the burdens for everyone, but I could see our situation as a problem or a challenge; and I had watched way too many John Wayne movies to not lead the way.

Leaders understand the value of attitude. There is no vaccination or injection someone can give you that contains attitude. Your attitude is inside of you and it will always be inside of you. It's there, in your heart and mind, you just need to sow the seeds of attitude to be able to reap the product of attitude. We need to plant it, cultivate it, fertilize it and when its time, to reap it. Attitude is a choice. Leaders find ways to develop and maintain their attitude. Some people build relationships to help them maintain a great attitude. While others read books, providing them with wisdom and knowledge on creating a good attitude. Some people place themselves in an environment where they are surrounded by people who know the importance of attitude.

Not one person on our backpack trip got poison ivy, sprained an ankle or broke a bone. Was there complaining and moaning during the trip, absolutely. I did my very best to not let what was happening on the outside of me, get on the inside of me. The part I remember best was that the sun was clearly shining at the end of our trip and ten students and two adults learned a weekend of lessons. Determine your attitude and win the day and never give up on your people.

NUGGET # 11

NO SOCKS

When I titled this chapter, I am referring to not letting our faithful companion play with or chew socks. I find it's a great temptation to roll several old socks into another sock, tie the end in a knot, and make a wonderful new play toy.

Unfortunately, most dogs cannot tell the difference between a good, still wearable sock and an old holey one ready for the rag bin. It was amazing how Chilli managed to locate every sock in the house that was left on the floor. However, the socks were not always old and tattered, more often than not they were new and expensive.

With the amount of dog toys on the market today, it's much easier for the pup to understand what a toy is and what isn't a toy. Hence, Nugget # 11:

"NO SOCKS"

It's not that socks are a terrible toy for pup to have, what we are talking about here is a "code of conduct."

With "No Socks" we're trying to teach the pup what toys are hers and what belongs to her master. In any relationship or team there's an importance to understanding a "code of conduct". This code of conduct is a set of values, expectations and boundaries which outlines the values, expectations and boundaries of those on the team.

As leaders, we need to establish a code of conduct right from the beginning of every adventure. It's much easier to live by the code of conduct from the start than to try to enforce it halfway through the journey. Let's apply the "No Sock" principle to everyday life.

The Bronx Zoo was our destination for a one-day family vacation. Living about three hours west of New York City, our journey began at 05:00 am. Both of our sons slept most of the way, which is usually the case for early morning departures for children. Arriving approximately one hour early we were the first car in line at the entrance to the zoo gates on that eventful morning. My wife and I and the boys were ready to escape from the confinements of our vehicle after this long ride. Even the outside of the zoo was beautiful compared to the inside of the car through the windshield.

Our boys were 8 and 4 years old at the time, and both of them had plenty of energy to release as they opened the car doors and quickly hit the sidewalk. After stretching a bit and complaining of the long ride, we found a park bench closest to the car and rested until the gates opened. My wife and I were happy just sitting there, watching other cars line up behind ours. Each vehicle held a family anxiously awaiting to be allowed into the zoo.

With my wife and I discussing the days travel through the zoo, we heard a sudden, sharp and loud "thwack!" Evidently our oldest son was bored and decided to throw stones to keep his time occupied. I am not sure what he was aiming at or for, but apparently, he hit the passenger side window on the car immediately behind ours. The lady sitting in the passenger seat was busy nursing a baby. As she screamed in terror and anger, her husband ejected from the driver's side door and was preparing to give both my son and me a tongue lashing.

With my heart in my hands, my son and I approached the gentlemen and immediately apologized. The gentlemen did accept my apologies, I am not so sure about his wife, as she returned to feeding her baby but still watched our son out of the corner of her eye. On this day we learned the importance of setting expectations and boundaries.

Leaders understand the importance of a code of conduct. This code, which is sometimes unwritten, is a set of values which each of us already have inside of us. One might call them the "do's and don'ts" of how to get along with others. Each of us have expectations of how we want to be treated and how we should treat others. Whether in a one-on-one conversation or in a large group meeting, when everyone understands what each person values, then teamwork truly begins to happen.

Values like dependability, honesty, integrity, trust and respect need to be established, understood and accepted before any team accomplishes its goal/s. When each of us agrees to and lives by an accepted code of conduct, a value system is established both internally and externally. When we value others for who they are, trust is formed, relationships grow and new ideas are shared freely and often improved upon.

It's up to you and I as leaders, to establish a code of conduct for our lives and for those relationships around us. When we value others for who they are and not who we want them to be, both our lives and the lives of others are enriched. John C. Maxwell tells us *"Every day value people, everyday think of ways to value people, everyday look for ways to value people and everyday encourage others to add value to people!"*

Sort of sounds like the Ten Commandments, doesn't it? Guess I should look at the Moses' stone list again and see what values I need to add to my code of conduct!

NUGGET # 12

INCH BY INCH

I find it amazing how much a Labrador retriever loves to run. It takes mere seconds for one of these breeds to travel the length of a football field. Huckleberry, our fox red male Labrador, travels even faster from his dog bed to the kitchen upon hearing the microwave door slam or the crackling of a plastic bag or even the refrigerator door opening. Dogs have incredible senses; sight, smell, sound, taste and even touch, a dog's smeller can locate one drop of oil in one million drops of water.

Whether Labrador retrievers or any breed of dog for that matter hears a familiar sound, smelling an odor or seeing an object they wish to have, their body stiffens, their ears perk up and their eyes widen with the thought of a treat. When we are training our house companions, whether at home or in the field, as their leader we want to use these senses to our advantage. Often in their training, I need to remind myself it's not about the speed in which our pup learns, but also how they move from one simple command to more complex commands. Thus, we need to apply Nugget # 12:

"INCH BY INCH!"

It's easy to get caught up moving forward in their learning, without their learning the current command 100 percent. By 100 percent, I mean, when we give the command "sit" the dog sits 100 percent of the time. Not most of the time, not some of the time, but 100 percent of the time. Sure, no dog is perfect, but our goal should be to have our pup perform the behavior to the best of their ability. We need to remember that lapses in their memory or even mistakes happen at times.

In today's world at the speed of a text message, growing and learning still needs a solid foundation. This foundation, like a concrete sidewalk, needs time to cure and strengthen. A puppy doesn't start with a large retrieving bumper. They start with a puppy bumper, a smaller one that fits in their mouth appropriately and then graduates to a larger training bumper as he grows bigger. Then as he matures, he would progress to where they can handle more advanced behavioral training.

Think of it like a kindergartener going to first grade and beyond. He shouldn't advance to the next grade until he conquers the current grade. A seven-month-old pup does not act like a seven-year-old dog. He can't.

When training your pup, others or even yourself, remember this famous phrase "Inch by inch, it's a cinch, yard by yard, it's very hard!" Like Rome, my leadership skills weren't built in a day and neither was my maturing process in 66 years. "Growing up" involved a matter of steps, and often those steps were incremental and methodical to achieve a predetermined goal.

Once I applied this Nugget to my dogs, I found it easy to utilize it in real life experiences. It may be just me, but it seems like knee replacements are about as common as going to the dentist for a root canal. Neither of these two experiences I look forward to. But I must say, when it came to therapy and my road to recovery for my first knee replacement, the PT kept recommending me to take one step at a time on my road to recovery.

One never forgets the first time you wake from a knee replacement surgery. I remember saying "this isn't so bad!" Until the pain medications wore off and the anesthesia left my body. As in most cases, the throbbing started out very soft and slow and built over the next several hours. The nurses had placed two buttons for me to push which were attached to the side of my bed. One for assistance and one for additional pain medicine. Over the next several hours I pressed both buttons pretty often, ok, very often and very hard, pressing hard didn't really help.

The doctor arrived in my room before dinner time, informing me how well the procedure went and he was adamant that I will need to be up and walking the next morning. Yeah, right! Accidents seemed to follow me wherever I went in life, whether motorcycles, chainsaws or bicycles. So, I knew from this procedure there would be no walking by me today, tomorrow or for a couple of days. Yeah, right!

Quickly the next morning, the nurse very abruptly informed me that therapy was happening in the rec room down the hall, and I was to be there in 15 minutes. Yeah, right!

At this point I couldn't feel my knee, leg or foot, but over the side of the bed, I threw my leg (which is Pennsylvania Dutch talk) and with a walker and two nurses, one on each side, down the hall I went at the speed of molasses in January!

There were four of us in the rec room, all leaning back on our recliners waiting for instructions. Evidently, the surgical room yesterday was very busy. I will say at this point the only thing I remember from the surgery was the thump of a severe pounding on

101

my left leg. Didn't hurt. Heck, I didn't even realize what was happening. But this morning I felt the aftereffects and now therapy was to begin.

During my journey of recovery over the next 7 weeks, I would progress from a week of therapy at home on my own, to three times a week at the therapy center. Slowly but surely, each day brought more bend in my knee, not much, just a small amount. I soon learned that "inch by inch, it's a cinch." For the first four weeks, we took it slow and steady performing the stretching, stepping and walking exercises until I graduated to a stationary bike, which, at first seemed impossible, but every day, little by little my knee became more bendable.

Leaders understand the principle of small steps lead to great achievements. Much like my physical therapy we need to apply this same principle in our own personal leadership growth and coaching and mentoring others. The next time you have a huge hurdle in front of you, break the project into small steps. Accomplish them one at a time, realize the accomplishment you just made and use this as motivation for the next step.

Think of the things in your life you like to do the least but are absolutely necessary. Maybe it's a new job position, a new job assignment, a new system to learn and install, or a new tool which came out that revolutionizes the way we have done things in the past. At times they can seem insurmountable. Instead of eating the whole Grandma's Black Chocolate cake with peanut butter icing all at once, cut off a small chunk, and enjoy it one bite at a time. Once a goal has been identified, establish the steps necessary to reach the goal. You just might be surprised how good it tastes and how easy you progress.

NUGGET # 13

LOW FENCES FIRST

It's easy to get excited as your dog learns new and exciting behaviors. Sit, stay, off, here and down are learned pretty quickly by a pup. Whether you use treats or praise for a reward, a six-month-old puppy learns very fast. At twelve months, it even seems faster.

At this point, please understand we don't move our dog's training along faster than the speed of their capabilities. Even though the dog is now learning

105

disciplined behaviors and doing amazing tricks while listening to our commands, we need to remember he's not ready for the big leagues, just yet.

Training our newly adopted friend should begin the very same day we bring them home or, at least the very next day. Each day, as he accelerates through the paces, it's important to remember he's not a super dog just yet. You want to build up his confidence so he becomes consistent in what he has achieved up to this point. If the dog fails on just one command, that's reason enough to stop and analyze if he's really as reliable as you might think in performing the act you are teaching. It's important to not move his training vertically until he has accomplished the task at hand.

Each day of training should build upon the previous days training. Not necessarily achieving a new task every day, but through repetition your pup becomes what we call steady or reliable.

I love Nugget # 13:

"LOW FENCES FIRST!"

Learning this discipline first, I am the one who needs to understand how my best friend becomes the best version of themselves that they can be. Whether as a dog or a human, great tasks are not accomplished until the not-so-great tasks are mastered. Learning and mastering the small tasks and challenges creates an environment of success and leads your dog up the ladder to more advanced learned behaviors. This step-by-step approach or shall I say raising the height of the bars on the fence, is not much different than going from elementary to middle to junior high and finally to senior high school and onto college.

Leaders understand the importance for creating and following a game plan. Whether the game plan is training your canine to be a favorable house guest or using this nugget for your own advancement, creating an environment or atmosphere is the first step on the ladder to success. I find it so easy to just live day by day and hope that what we learned thru the childhood years and school, have helped me become a better leader. Not so! There is so much information and so much to learn about the world, I need to challenge my perceived wisdom.

Growing up, I tended to believe what everyone said was the truth, that doctors know all the answers to medical questions and even that I have the best answer for every question. This is just not so. I find that the more I learn, the more I find out what I didn't know about leadership. John C. Maxwell tells us *"Leadership is influence!"* There are many definitions by many great leaders and speakers, but this one hits me right between the eyes. Right to my very core. I thought leaders were the people in charge, in whatever field or endeavor in life. When I started applying the word influence as a verb instead of a noun, it was like someone tried to feed me dog food. No way was I eating that stuff.

As I read more books on leadership, as I asked others what leadership means to them, my thought process changed. I wanted to learn more. When I began dog training under the mentorship of a seasoned, veteran dog trainer, my perceived wisdom about dogs and their training was challenged, if not changed. My thoughts about how to train a dog, in fact, were nothing at all what I expected. One of the best decisions I have made in my life, was to seek the help of a mentor. I needed to spend time with him, listen and learn, to respect him and I needed a willingness to change.

When I first met my newly established mentor, I wasn't expecting to learn life's lessons of leadership. But did I ever. It was a fantastic two-year journey.

This gentleman provided me with an environment in understanding dogs. His knowledge of dogs and dog behavior was simply mystifying to me. Each day we spent together, I returned with a confidence that I could be an accomplished dog trainer. There are times when he challenged me with questions and I can honestly say that when I arrived to spend the day with him and his dogs, he was ready to hit the field, excited and encouraging. I loved his humility, honesty and consistency. Little did I know at the time, that I was helping him with training the dogs in his camp for others, he was training me on more than animal behavior. His mentorship/relationship provided me with a new perspective, a different outlook and helped me create a very meaningful relationship with my training companion.

As you can tell, my mentor holds a very special place in my heart that will never leave. Much like training dogs, he was helping me to jump low fences first. My two-year journey with him was built upon an environment, one in which I could learn at my speed of learning. As I began to add more rails to the fence, my confidence grew and my willingness to accept new challenges grew. Each day I spent with this truly one-of-a-kind mentor, along with my four-legged training partner, were some of the best days of my life.

Each of us have memories of our past that leave a forever lasting feeling in our hearts. The sight of your dog achieving its first title at an event or the sound they make when you are leaving the house without them. Maybe it's the touch of their cold nose or the look in their eyes when their head tilts as if to say, "why are you doing that?" These are memories that stick with us that will always be remembered.

Leaders find ways to create an environment for others to learn, to feel comfortable and safe. When we truly value others for who they are and not who we want them to be, a climate is created. This climate must be established and maintained by each of us. Whether we are in charge or in someone else's charge, each of us are responsible for climate control. This environment doesn't automatically appear or exist, each of us needs to take ownership of our lives in order to live a successful life. Just as I was mentored, cared for and taught, we must do the same for those we have been given responsibility over, raising those rails when needed or keeping them at the same height for a period of time.

In the evening after a long day of dog training, my wife would say "I smell a wet dog!" To me, the smell tells me that my dog and I have created a relationship that will forever last in my nose and heart. Each of us have learned to jump low fences first.

NUGGET # 14

TO BE UNCLEAR IS

TO BE UNKIND

Have you found yourself scolding your dog after he finally listens to what you wanted him to do?

I remember a loveable yellow, extra-large, male Labrador retriever named Levi that we owned and a nasty little habit he had. He would often wander down the sidewalks in our small town (which is really another matter of me not being responsible for my dog). Sometimes he would be a half a block down the street, and when I saw him, I would call his name. He would turn and stare at me with that wonderful, tender, smiling face and give me the look that said, "That's me, stop yelling my name!" I would call his name repeatedly as he just stood there looking at me, probably thinking "Hey, dad has a treat for me, I might as well go see what he has for me!"

The last thought I had on my mind was giving the rascal a treat. Trying to keep my cool, I watched him as he moseyed back to me (I love the word moseyed). When he would finally reach me, I would give him a scolding for not listening. He thought I gave him a tongue lashing for returning to me.

I needed to understand and apply Nugget # 14:

"TO BE UNCLEAR IS TO BE UNKIND!"

116

It had suddenly dawned on me that my dog's thought pattern was totally different than mine and I needed to learn to understand his way of thinking. I also needed to learn how to understand and connect with Levi. Levi being a dog which doesn't speak human and me being a human which doesn't speak dog, you can see the predicament. He may have been thinking *Dude, I just came to you and now you are not happy with me? Get a grip, human!"* In my mind, I thought he was disobeying a command. Like most cases with my dog training tactics, I was the one who needed to learn the most. If I was going to communicate with Levi, I needed to change my way of communicating. Whenever communication fails to be effective, I must first ask myself, "What did I do to cause a miscommunication and what can I do differently to help make the message clear."

After 25 years of working in a coal fired power plant, learning how to make electricity, I decided a change was in order for my life and my career. The opportunity arose to work at a service center, where linemen keep the flow of electricity going to homeowners and businesses. Now, completely out of my element of producing electricity, I dove into a world which involved bucket trucks, line crews and a whole plethora of terminology I had never heard of. Poles, transformers, capacitors, tap fuses, cut out switches and drip loops. These common names of hardware were common in the service center, but not to someone who was new to a completely different line of work.

Leaders are *communicators*, some people are born with naturally good communication skills and others, well, let's just say there are a lot of words which could be added to their vocabulary, if they choose to. My position at the service center was dispatcher, the guy who receives trouble calls from customers out of power and uses a radio to direct the linemen where to go to find the problem in a town, city or in the rural countryside. These linemen are travelling with all kinds of equipment needed to restore power to those in need. Their bucket trucks must have hundreds of tools and pieces of equipment.

One such day, I was directing several line crews to a location to restore power to the surrounding homes and farms when after several hours, one of the linemen in that location calls me on the radio for some help. When you are sitting in an office, miles away from the location of the power outage, there is no way anyone can tell what the situation, predicament or trouble the line crews might have found. Using the radio to communicate from their location back to the service center, I hear the following message. "I need a pole!" I quickly answered and asked them what size pole they needed. Utility poles come in many different sizes to meet the weight of the load they are holding up. I replied, "What size pole would you like me to have delivered to your job site?" The answer came back across the radio "No

Caz, I need a pole!" Huh? They didn't give me the answer I wanted to supply them with what they need. I replied again "What size pole do you need?!" Both my temper and the linemen's temper were starting to heat up as our communication really wasn't connecting accurately. Finally, the crew leader takes the microphone on the radio and reports "Caz, we are stuck in the mud, we need a pull!" When one visits another area country, it's always the other person which has an accent, not us. Yeah, right. The words coming from the radio were clear enough, I just was not hearing what they were saying.

This linemen lingo was all new to me. I was used to words like pumps, fans, turbines, boilers and motors. Now I was in a world which had their own way or style of speaking. I can tell you that I am the type of person who can take a good joke, and believe me, when communicating via a radio, the entire service center heard our conversation and so did every line crew within ear shot. The crews just couldn't wait to get back to the barn, park their line trucks and bust into the office to rib me with all their power and skill. We all had a great laugh, but I learned a tremendous lesson that day.

Leaders are perpetual learners. Every day, there is something new to learn, ***if we choose to learn it.*** There are natural born leaders and there are those of us, who learn, and apply leadership principles every-day. My wife will sit for hours and read books; she is a natural born reader. As for me, not so much. In high school, I read zero number of books. Did every book report from the inside cover of the book and didn't understand the importance of reading and preparing book reports. At age 17, I figured why should I read, I already know all there is to know.

Being a good communicator is a learnable skill. While some are natural born, others need to invest in themselves by reading, studying other communicators and practice. Good communication is more than just fancy or intricate words and definitions. Good communication starts with a desire to learn to become better at connecting with others. Leaders become great communicators when they see value in the ones they are communicating with. Everyone can grow their communication skills if they choose to.

NUGGET # 15

TEACH LESS, LEARN MORE!

When I first started retriever training, I began to see great improvements each day. Both myself and my canine companion were gaining confidence in each other and we really began to work as a team. I can't really say whether I thought I was a great trainer or they were great dogs. Soon, I started to realize that both of us were learning and the dogs were much more naturally capable of learning than I was in training them.

On my days off work, I found myself trying to cram one or two hours of training into segments of fifteen minutes. Cramming their training like this didn't work, neither for the dog or for me. The entire process beginning from home to training field and back was better performed when each of us were not hurried. I needed to prepare myself for every training session by deciding what I want the pup to learn during their training session.

When thinking through every step in the pup's training and writing it down in a journal, this becomes the first step in the process of learning these new behaviors. Often, I refer to their feats of magic as newly learned behaviors. We might call them tricks; I prefer to call them behaviors due to the fact that each dog is beginning to reach their full potential. Adding at this point the principle of Nugget # 15:

"TEACH LESS, LEARN MORE"

This Nugget applies not only to our dogs but to us as well. Our training session when our trainee was just a 6-month-old pup, began by getting them excited over the sight of the retrieving bumper. Next, we proceeded to getting her to love this newfound training tool. After a week or two of fun and games, we proceeded to more serious training. Here is the time to start interjecting new words and commands into their training. Each training event from here on out was much more disciplined and structured. Each training endeavor needs to be much more organized, thought out and even controlled.

127

The basis or foundation for the principle of "teach less, learn more" applies to both dogs and humans alike. It's very easy to have pup retrieve tennis balls or training bumpers dozens of times poorly, because they often play the game of come catch me. I would rather have them complete three retrieves on command done well, as to dozens of retrieves where our buddy might be very sloppy in the three phases of a retrieve: sit by my side, retrieve the object on command and return to me with the object. Sloppiness on their part in training, breeds laziness and disobedience in their effort. There is a saying often repeated in the wrestling room "perfect practice instills perfect behavior."

Learning this lesson in life helps others to learn, it also brings great satisfaction to the teacher/leader. Learning doesn't happen in just one day, it needs to happen every day. I quickly discovered as I learned these Nuggets, that teaching less really means learning more.

I still remember as a small child learning to swim. I was not thrown into the water with the idea of sink or swim. My father started my learning by teaching the basics of swimming in the Susquehanna River. First, he taught me how to float. Second, I learned how to doggy paddle and then, the overhand stroke. I did not learn all of these three basics the first time out. Each time we went for an evening swim, I learned in steps and I did not advance to the next step until I learned the current step he was teaching.

No wonder by the time I was a teenager, I was already beginning to swim like a fish. In fact, one couldn't get me out of the water from pool opening to closing time. During my swimming lessons and learning, not once did I attempt the difficult steps before learning the basic steps. Nor did I ever jump off the low diving board before jumping into the waiting arms of my parents or sister. The high dive, well that took a lot of confidence and courage before I attempted that scary death-defying feat.

Leaders help others reach their full potential by understanding this Nugget. A swimmer floats before they swim and they swim before they dive. The greatest of all divers and the fastest of all swimmers learned to be great at their craft by learning the steps necessary to be successful. They master the first step or lesson before moving onto more difficult ones. Once a step or achievement is mastered on the current step of learning, then and only then do they move onto the next step. Not accomplishing each step in the learning process will ensure dissatisfaction in our capabilities and give us pause upon tackling the next challenge.

I often find myself wanting to take the steps at a faster pace or maybe even thinking I am doing a task well enough to move on, but this will bring less than perfection for the next step. This really is important, you know. A few shortcuts here and a small loss of efficiency there and upon reaching the higher steps we set ourselves up for a failure. Being brilliant in the basics is about teaching less so that we understand more, then we will learn more. Todays' small steps lead to tomorrow's great achievements.

NUGGET # 16

ALWAYS BELIEVE IN YOUR DOG!

Believing in yourself is a powerful feeling, which not everyone does. Neither does every dog. Even though this belief is an inner feeling, it's often dependent on how others look at the dog, at us, and how they treat the dog or us and share with the dog or us.

Believing in your dog should be a personal philosophy formed even before owning, training and living with them. When a dog feels that his human

133

believes he or she is the best dog in the world, their life and behavior shines. When the dog's owner/leader comes in the door of their home, the dog's tail wags, his ears perk up and his excitement level is off the charts. Your dog feels from his inner depth that he is loved and knows he is a part of the family unit, not just a pet. We often believe our companions think they are humans, when in fact I believe most of the time, they believe we are dogs. Think about it.

To show my dog that I believe in him means that I will prepare, plan and expect the pup to accomplish the task and challenges that lies ahead of him.

Thus, I formulated Nugget # 16:

"Always believe in you dog!"

Our often-challenging companions easily recognize whether or not their human has faith in them. Our belief in them or may we interject the words, faith in them, is clearly evident by their eye contact, the position of their ears, the tilt of their head and even the wag of their tails.

Many times, in our training exercises, when I throw a training bumper for him to find, whether in a field, the woods or even floating in water, I need to learn to let my dog keep looking for the object to retrieve. We often want to step in and help them find the object but letting them accomplish the retrieve or

135

any task does more for their confidence and self-worth than giving treats, letting him chew on socks or allowing him to do whatever he wants.

I admit I'm getting a little sentimental here, but I've learned that time and energy, or the lack thereof, quickly determines the strength of a relationship. As a leader, believing in those you surround yourself with, not only helps them become better, but it also builds their faith in you. With faith comes trust, and trust should be the foundation of all relationships.

Leaders realize the importance of having faith in those around them. When we truly believe in someone, it shows from the inside of us and the outside of us. Having faith in others should be a personal philosophy, a standard operating procedure

(SOP's) of the way we live our lives. Honesty, dependability, and trustworthiness are a few of the SOP's that each of us need to establish in our own lives. When we establish this personal philosophy, feed and grow ourselves with information and application, our self-image grows. Do I see myself as a person of value? Then and only then, will we truly value others for who they are, and not for who we want them to be.

This personal philosophy that we need to develop is who we truly are on the inside. We have all learned to be who we are thru nature and nurture; this should not limit us from becoming more each day. What the word 'more' means is different to each of us. Wanting to write this book for at least 10 years, my wife believed in me more than I ever did. Her belief in me has given me the confidence to complete this book and to write many, many more.

Let me share more. All home projects should begin before they are started. Think about it, an idea lights up in our brain, ok, maybe in my wife's brain. Her thinking or better yet, her disciplined thinking stirs a discussion and before you know it, we are at the dining room table explaining ideas and eventually writing them down on paper. Once we have decided on what and how we are going to do something, we set about putting the steps in place to accomplish the task.

Amazing how over the 46 years of marriage, she often knows me better than I know myself. Even when I think I know the answer to all of life's problems or situations. I really believe this is why the saying "opposites attract" is a very important philosophy to understand. I am 6'3' and she is 5'3" She is very patient and I am well, not so patient. When we see each other for who we are, we accomplish great things together. Marriage requires a personal philosophy. She needs to have one, I need to have one and we need to have one together. She is a natural born listener while I am a natural born talker. She loves to hear stories and I love to share stories. Both of these behaviors we were born with, but that doesn't mean we cannot each learn from each other and "adapt, improvise and overcome" as Clint Eastwood reports to his platoon in **Heart Break Ridge.**

I guess I could have named this chapter "Always believe in your wife!" What a great personal philosophy to have in life. This belief in your spouse takes time and energy. It takes trials and tribulations. I didn't understand this philosophy when we first got married. I often wanted things with the saying "it's my way or the highway!" I can say that after 46 years of marriage, we still have arguments, challenges and more. We often want things our own way. Some of our most confusing decisions have been over where to go for supper on Friday night.

In a marriage, when each spouse believes in each other, and has the same personal philosophy about marriage, great things happen. Each person has their own unique personality. Our personality was given to us by God, intentionally, on purpose, with a design for our lives. God designed our personality but our behaviors are what we continually need to work on and our personal philosophy of how we treat ourselves and others. One of the very most important behaviors or qualities in life, is to have faith. To have faith, we need to believe in those who we have identified as trustworthy, dependable, consistent, honest and more. We decide what our personal philosophy is before an event happens. Before the situation arises and challenges us to make a decision. Leaders understand the value of having faith in others.

142

NUGGET # 17

REPETITION IS THE

MOTOR OF LEARNING

What you repetitively do becomes your standard behavior. Hmmm! How poignant the thought when working with your faithful companion? It only takes pup a couple times to hear the "beep" of the microwave, the sound of the dog treat jar lid being removed or the sound of the fridge door opening to have them come running. Whether they are sound asleep, at the opposite end of the yard or in a room with a blasting TV, the dog's reaction is more of a Spiderman "tingly sense" that they possess.

143

Utilizing Nugget # 17:

"Repetition is the Motor of Learning"

I quickly accelerated our dog's entire training regimen. I would shake the treat container, (which became a sound they will never forget) call their name, have them sit, give them praise and a doggie treat and "voila!" This newly found repetitive lesson taught all of our dogs to sit, stay and shake, very quickly. Correctly doing a repetitive act for two or more days, the dogs had it perfected. Often raising their paw to shake even before the rattle of the treat container or given the command, I must have looked like a magician at times to my wife and children. We often found our four-legged companions sitting below the counter where upon the jar of heavenly morsels was positioned. Hungry or not hungry, I am sure their regular dog food was more like the food we give our babies from a baby food jar. They loved their food, but treats, well that was a whole different ecstasy.

The importance of repetition really was one of the most important factors of increasing my knowledge of dog training. I found the more time I spent with my mentor (pro dog trainer) the more knowledgeable and adept that I became in training dogs. This repetitiveness really was the key to instilling more and more dog knowledge into me than I realized. With repeating certain dog exercises over and over again, what I was learning was being instilled into my memory bank, forever. Ok, for quite a long time.

Along with being repetitive in my association with my mentor, I began to read books about dogs.

As much as I want my children and grandchildren to read every day, I must confess that there are days I do not read. Leaders choose to make reading a consistent, repetitive discipline. Here is how I started my reading regimen.

- I began looking for dog books that drew my interest.
- I chose to read dog books which helped me understand dog behaviors.
- I read books about dog breeds, behaviors and how to train them.

146

One of my very favorite books on dogs is entitled "The Art of Raising a Puppy" by The Monks of New Skete. I devoured this book in two sessions. Yes, it only took me two evenings to read it. After reading my first book, I wanted to read another. And another! And another!

Repetition is the motor of learning. Now everything we read might not be true or be pertinent to each of us. The first key of importance in repetition was finding books that interest and intrigue you. The more information I devoured about canines and their world, the more I wanted to read and learn. The second key of importance in repetition here is that the more I read, the more I wanted to read. This continued education brought about more training and growth for my best friend. The third key of importance in repetition is taking action.

It was one thing to learn about dogs and their behaviors but it was a completely different issue when applying it to their training. One can read about how to ride a bicycle, but one doesn't really know how to ride until they...... get on the bike and wreck a few times. Like getting back on the horse, once we are bucked off. I made plenty of mistakes when training my retrievers to do their lifelong passion. Adjusting from my mistakes and applying these corrections repetitively has helped me grow as a leader and a dog trainer.

As trust is the foundation of leadership, building trust with our canine companions, friends, co-workers and families grows when we repeatedly do what we say we will do, fulfilling our commitments on time and are honest with both ourselves and others.

I remember going to fire fighting school many years ago, and this kind of training is not a once and done endeavor. Each year I went to fire school and learned different techniques and knowledge in the world of firefighting. One small but important part of the training was in knot tying. At one time my knot tying skills were let's say "can't tie a knot, tie a lot!" Which meant to just keep tying overhand knots until one felt the knot would not come loose.

When it comes to different kinds of knots, there must be dozens and dozens, each one serving a different purpose. To learn these different knots like:

149

bowline, half hitch, figure eight and many more is not an easy task. How does one learn and remember each of them? By repeating the act of tying them over and over and over again. Repetition! Not just tying them hundreds of times in a day, but tying them many times for many days as it takes to master the process. Leadership is built on trust and trust is like a muscle which must be exercised. The instructor demonstrated many times how to tie these knots, although not until I repetitively tied them over and over, was it that I truly mastered the art of knot tying.

As a leader, we build trust by being consistent in our actions and our words. Always telling the truth is another example of what each of us can repetitively do to grow our leadership skills. Others will rely on us when we are truthful. I learned this lesson one day at the power plant where I was currently working. During an abnormal startup of the units an incident occurred. A person disconnected the wrong switch while making repairs and shut down the entire power plant, what we call a "trip!" Whew! Everyone was on the move to get power back on line and restored to the power grid. The gentleman who made the mistake, immediately admitted that he was the one who made the mistake. I will never forget his honesty. He was one who I could always depend on for the truth. This type of honesty requires a personal philosophy and it is developed by repetitvely being honest, all the time.

I can't imagine any team working together at their peak, without the team members being consistent and repetitive in their actions. Can you image how many times a pitcher has practiced throwing baseballs? How many hours a pianist has spent at the piano or how many hours a seamstress has spent in front of their sewing machines? Very seldom do we get proficient at any skill without repetitively spending a great deal of time and energy at the task we are learning to master.

Repetition is a muscle which needs to be exercised and used. It's up to us to understand and use this tool in order for ourselves to grow to our full potential as leaders. What we repetitively do, we become.

NUGGET # 18

NO WHINING

ALLOWED

It's amazing the amount of sounds a pup can make. We humans naturally place a meaning to each and every one, correctly or incorrectly. The same as looking in a dog's eyes when we're eating a meal, we associate what his heart's desire is. Out of all the sounds a dog can make, I find whining translates into one of the most important leadership lessons to learn.

153

How do you respond when your dog is whining? With retriever training, it's very common to have my dog sit and wait until I give the "fetch" command. This scenario begins with a training session, on a field of grass and weeds. I want my dog to retrieve an object that has just been thrown by my assistant (in this case my uncle). My expectation is for my Labrador retriever to watch the object being thrown into the air, sit by my side very still and very quiet and wait for the "fetch" command. Upon hearing the word fetch, he is to leave my side, run to the object, pick it up and hold it in his mouth and return to my left side. Pretty simple. Pup has done it 1,000 times in practice.

But today, he is really keyed up. Meaning he is excited and just can't wait to do the work I need him to do. So, his emotions get the best of him, his heartbeat is elevated, his desire is off the charts and now those inner sounds of excitement are expressed in what we call "whining". During the training or even in the field as a working dog, our wish is for this field companion to be exceptionally quiet. Get the picture. They are so excited with anticipation that they just can't keep quiet.

At this point if I let my dog whine first and complete the retrieve, I have taught him that it's okay to make these very soft sounds when training and what they learn in training becomes their second nature. Upon watching him and hearing him whine, I immediately use the words "hush" or quiet"! If my pup understands the hush command and quiets himself, then and only then will I allow him to make the retrieve. If he stays noisy and actually is disobeying my command, I need to get him to calm down and stop whining. Often, this is accomplished by redirecting his thinking. I might walk him at heel in a small circle to change his mental picture or I might have my assistant retrieve the bumper and we start the exercise again. Get the picture?

I guess I should better clarify what whining is and isn't. When my four-legged companion is whining, he is not willing to be completely obedient. He is wanting his own way. He is overriding me as his master/leader. Whining is a dog's favorite method to get his own way. The behavior isn't always bad except when done repetitively, which eventually builds and escalates into an annoying, incessant and irritating attention getter. If your pup learns to whine whenever they want something, they will always whine to get their own way like wanting to be on the couch, bed, chair, or their owner's lap. While most dog owners enjoy a nudge from their pups when they want their human's attention, ten minutes of whining, begging or pleading is not an acceptable behavior.

Enter Nugget # 18:

"NO WHINING ALLOWED!"

Ever gone shopping at the supermarket only to hear a child whining for a different grocery item in each aisle? Once the parent gives in on the first whine, guess what that child has learned to do? Yup, whine, and they can get pretty darn good at it. Their whining can go from a small tilt of the head and a look of don't you love me anymore to a full-blown repetition of please, please, please, please and many more to follow. If we ignore the incessant whining, we are telling our child that it's okay to keep doing it. They also learn that every time they want something, they know exactly what to do to get their own way. You know, pulling your strings.

A leader is a connector of people. They have many acquaintances, advocates, allies and friends who have helped them along their leadership journey. They have mentors and coaches who were willing to help them learn to become better leaders. Raising a family at the age of 20, I found myself thinking or believing I knew all the answers to parenthood. Hey, I watched what other parents do and I definitely do not want to go down that road, LOL. As a newlywed and starting out with a family at such a young age, I quickly found out I had much to learn about raising children.

I now understand the reason we have books written by authors like Dr. Dobson who founded Focus on the Family and many others. Raising children is easy to talk about and often easy to understand, but to carry out these lessons in real life with a 4-year-old, that's another story. Until one walks this pathway of parenting, one never really quite understands the challenges of parenthood. Oh, I can easily see the mistakes in other parents at the grocery store but carrying out these leadership lessons in my own life, that's another story.

I hope by now, by reading this book you have taken notice that each Nugget affects all the other Nuggets. They do not stand alone. Each application, each story and each principle actually are tied together which makes them so much more powerful than standing by themselves. Learning these leadership lessons in conjunction with their applications, well, I hope you see that it is much easier said than done.

Each of my dogs have learned from their previous house guests. They have watched each other get in trouble, get corrected and learned from each other. With one dog watching another, much is learned or as they say, more is caught than is taught. Whether it is inside the house, or outside in their playing yard or training in the field, every one of my dogs learned many behaviors by watching each other. Probably the best picture of learning from others is taking them as a small pup to the creek and letting them play with their canine playmates. Doesn't take long until that precious little pup is doing the doggy paddle like a champion swimmer.

Can you imagine a 40-year-old husband coming up to his wife and whining over something he wants to purchase? Please, please, please, please! Nope, it ain't gonna happen. No whining allowed simply challenges each of us to manage our emotions and behaviors. Great leaders understand the importance of their emotions and the emotions of others which increased better communication and teamwork.

NUGGET # 19

IT'S ALL ABOUT THE EYES!

I'm not sure what it is about having a dog just stare at you eye to eye. Can that dog really see my pupils? Does he know I have hazel-colored eyes? Does he know when I'm looking at him or at the TV? Does he know I am talking about him without me even mentioning his name? Or do I know what he is seeing when he looks at me? Am I a T bone steak? Does he see me as his best friend with love and adoration or does he see me as someone who leaves

163

him alone all day in the house by himself, abandoning him five days a week? I believe all of the above could be answered with a "yes!"

Have you ever noticed that when you tell your pup the word "no" as he is eyeing a piece of food falling from the dinner table, he'll usually wait for your command if you're looking at him eye to eye? However, I've discovered when I look away from the dog then wham! He was on that scrap like the best steak he ever ate. The morsel could be cauliflower, broccoli or asparagus, he doesn't care what it is, he'll eat it. I will say some dogs, the pickier type eaters, might sniff it first and make a decision to gobble the morsel or not. But for my Labrador retrievers, there is no waiting for a good smell. If the piece of table scrap fell from that delicious plateau the dog is never allowed to be upon, there is no 5 second rule and their eyes tell the other dogs, first come, first served. He would then give me that look that said "I wasn't supposed to eat that? Really? I thought you did that on purpose!"

They would rather chomp first, then decide if it is actually stomach worthy. Notice I didn't say taste worthy? I call them *shovelers!* (*eat first, ask questions later*) These four-legged canine companions are *shovelers*. They will eat first, taste second and on rare occasions, be able to return the swallowed object from the pits of their stomach onto my wife's favorite rug. I shall not go any further just in case some of you reading this have queasy stomachs.

Those of us who are canine affectionate know what I am talking about. It's the look we get at night from our bedroom companions as they wait for human approval to jump onto the bed or the stare we received when we're leaving the house even if only to empty the trash, is a priceless gem of canine love. The amount of communication transmitted by watching each other's eyes is amazing, and again, this is not only true in the dog world.

As a developing leader, I am constantly reminding myself of Nugget # 19:

"IT'S ALL ABOUT THE EYES!"

Are you looking around the room right now, to see if anyone is watching you smile? We can read a lot about each other in our environment by watching their eyes, their facial expressions and the curve of their smile.

Recently my wife and I were watching one of the zillionth episodes of Friends. Like many classic hit TV shows, these relationship-oriented sitcoms, have so much more to offer than just entertainment. Whether its Mash, Seinfeld, The Big Bang Theory or Friends, one can watch the entire half hour episode with no sound coming from the television and we can still understand a lot of what is happening. Joy, fear, anger, disgust and sadness are but a few of the recognizable emotions we pick up on either intentionally or subliminally. As my wife and I were discussing the latest world news, I muted the television for this episode of Friends and soon found myself knowing exactly what was happening. Even though my wife and I were discussing a subject, each of us could observe what was happening on this episode. Someone was arguing, someone was afraid, someone was happy and still others were using their eyes to communicate either their pleasure or displeasure.

I should also reveal to the reader, that yes, if I was having a discussion with my wife and also monitoring the television, I wasn't really in the moment, was I? I was not giving her my full attention, but we will save that leadership lesson for my next book.

My leadership mentor told me "Walk slowly through the crowd!" Typically, I am the type "A" personality that upon arrival at the event, quickly reports "I am here!" You know my type. Outgoing, bubbly, full of stories and jokes. Ready to talk a lot and listen? Well not so much. But it's the eyes that really tell the story. It has been said that the eyes are the window to the soul.

One of the greatest characteristics of a leader is having the ability to truly understand people. To understand them, we need to observe them. The tilt of their head, the curl of their eyebrow and the purse of their lips. Their eyes often look up or down, or to the sides and even gaze into the upper atmosphere when their "tells" are revealing their feelings.

Why is this important for a leader to know and understand? To truly have empathy for one another, to truly desire to make a difference in the lives of others, we need to be observant of their emotions.

169

"Walking slowly thru the crowd" is what sticks in my head. Am I aware of the needs of others? Do I focus my conversation on them or on me? Do I simply nod my head and tell them I understand or do I truly want to know more about them? What causes them pain, sadness or happiness?

Leaders choose to be leaders and each one of us can build our leadership skills by grasping this Nugget and practicing it every day. When we get up in the morning and look in the mirror, we can see a lot about ourselves. The first step in knowing and understanding others, is to first know and understand ourselves.

Each day may seem like the same old routine. But in reality, each day presents a new opportunity, a new challenge for each of us to learn and grow.

Napoleon Hill writes in his book "Think and Grow Rich!" about the Sixth Sense, gaining Wisdom. At one time I believed that wisdom came with age. Today, I believe that my wisdom grows when my empathy grows.

The dictionary defines Empathy as: *the ability to understand and share the feelings of another.* Whether we are at home, social events, outdoor gatherings or a church social, leaders make a difference when they have empathy for others. For me, empathy means being in the moment and giving my full attention to the person in front of me.

I need to ask myself every day. Am I self-centered or am I others centered? This Nugget possibly should have been the first chapter. Then again, maybe not.

171

In 1 Samuel 16:7 it says: *But the LORD said to Samuel, "Do not consider his appearance or his height, for I have rejected him. The LORD does not look at the things people look at. People look at the outward appearance, but the LORD looks at the heart."*

Not all leaders will, but effective leaders do.

172

NUGGETS APPLIED

How many words or commands can a dog learn? As many as we are willing to teach them. When I learned this principle, my pup's and my own life changed. Each Nugget of this book can be applied not only to our salivating, barking, digging, chasing, growling, barking, running, always ready for a treat, four legged loved ones. They can and should also be applied to every area of our life.

What I have learned as an amateur dog trainer, I am now applying to every area of my life in growing my leadership skills! God uses many tools in life to help us become the best version of ourselves that we can be. It is also our responsibility to become the leader or leaders we were born to be, for our family, our friends and our neighbors. Leadership is a Choice! It begins with me and ends with me.

During the first few months of dog training, I didn't know much about canine behaviors. I didn't even have a clue. Oh, I thought I knew a lot about dogs and like those who love to learn, we find out how little we really know when we set out to learn more.

The ten years I spent with my mentor, whom I mentioned earlier in this book, went by so fast. With each Labrador retriever I trained, I learned more and more. It took me 66 years to get to the level of leadership skills I am currently at and I do not consider myself an expert, not even close. I hope you enjoyed reading this book as much as I did in writing it. Most of all, let every pup you come into contact with know that they are the best dog in the world. What a great leadership principle in life as we meet others and build relationships.

WHEN WE SHARE AND HELP OTHERS LEARN, WE TRULY LIVE LIVES THAT ARE SIGNIFICANT.

175

Made in the USA
Monee, IL
21 August 2021